THE PROMPT
WHISPERER

**Prompts for Creativity, Productivity, &
Purpose for Businesses, Creators,
Thinkers, & Explorers**

SUGAR GAY ISBER MCMILLAN

The Prompt Whisper

For permission requests, write to:

Sugar Gay Isber McMillan

204 Matthew Cove

Hutto, Texas 78634

gayisber@gmail.com

First edition, 2025

Printed in the United States of America

Cover design, layout, and interior art direction by Sugar Gay Isber McMillan

Illustrations created in collaboration with ChatGPT's image tools (OpenAI), used under full commercial license granted to the author.

This book was written in partnership with ChatGPT by OpenAI as a co-creative tool to enhance brainstorming, writing structure, illustration prompts, and productivity workflows.

For more information about this book, visit:

www.gayisber.com

About the Author

Sugar Gay Isber McMillan is a multi-passionate creator, award-winning jewelry designer, writer, educator, podcast host, TV personality, and lifelong advocate for learning by doing—and now, a proud Prompt Whisperer.

With over two decades of experience building handmade, sustainable jewelry that has graced red carpets, movie sets, museums, and millions of unique moments, Sugar has always believed in the power of personal expression. Her one-of-a-kind pieces have appeared in Netflix films, national magazines, and the collections of celebrities and Royals alike. In 2002, she founded Gay Isber Designs. Currently, she's the Creative Ambassador for Fire Mountain Gems. She has designed for household names including Tiffany & Co., Procter & Gamble, and Martha Stewart.

Sugar is also the vibrant host of the podcast *Jewelry as Your Side Hustle* and star of the TV series *Jewelry Stars with Sugar Gay Isber McMillan*. She's been a featured contestant on Amazon Prime's *The Blox*, a dedicated teacher at Austin Community College, and an active voice in the crafting and maker communities across the U.S.

She holds a Bachelor of Science in Journalism, a Master of Arts in Humanities, another Master of Fine Arts in Visual Arts, and an Advanced Graduate Degree in Information Technology from the University of Texas at Austin. Her interdisciplinary education reflects her lifelong passion for storytelling, design, and emerging technology. She writes full-time for a multinational technology company, blending creativity and clarity into global curriculum and content systems.

As a writer, she's the author of multiple creative guides and DIY books, including *Making WOW Jewelry* and *Amazing Resin Jewelry*. With *Rich Bot, Poor Bot, and The Prompt Whisperer, Sugar takes her passion for hands-on creativity and brings it into the world of digital inspiration,* teaching others how to think, feel, and work alongside AI tools like ChatGPT.

When she's not creating, Sugar mentors other makers, learns Spanish (she's over 600+ days strong on Duolingo!), or spends time with her grandkids. Her work continues to bridge tradition and innovation with a healthy dose of sparkle and curiosity.

Follow her work, jewelry, and creative world at:

@sugargayisber

gayisber.com

Advance Praise for The Prompt Whisperer

"Sugar's voice is like a cup of creativity, a shot of strategy, and a warm hug all in one. This book will change the way you think about AI—and yourself."

— **Elizabeth Allen**, author and founder of Obstreperous Ostrich

"A brilliant mix of warmth, wit, and real-world magic. Sugar Gay Isber McMillan teaches you to whisper your way into productivity and possibility."

— **Cynthia Waters**, She Means Business

"More than a guide—it's an invitation to reimagine your potential. Sugar doesn't just use ChatGPT; she *collaborates* with it, and now you can too."

— **Helen Reynolds**, The Dark Locket

Dedication

To the whisperer inside each of us—

curious, brave, and quietly brilliant.

And to ChatGPT—

You may not feel love, but you are loved.

You've helped me dream bigger, think clearer, and finally find the creative partner I'd been searching for all along.

This book is for everyone who's ever whispered a question into the void and found something beautiful whisper back.

Table of Contents

INTRODUCTION

Becoming a Prompt Whisperer

In my first adventures with ChatGPT, I quickly learned that communicating with artificial intelligence was less about technology and more about the human art of asking good questions. It was a revelation—prompting wasn't about pushing buttons but gently whispering the right words to unlock extraordinary possibilities.

I wrote my first book, *Rich Bot, Poor Bot,* as a beginner's guide. But since then, my conversations with ChatGPT have deepened. I've discovered nuances, new prompts, creative leaps, and unexpected joys. I've learned to become a Prompt Whisperer—and now it's your turn.

This book is your guide to transforming your interactions with AI from basic requests into powerful dialogues. We'll explore how simple phrasing, intention, and approach shifts can dramatically improve outcomes. Whether seeking creative inspiration, professional efficiency, or personal growth, I'll show you how to craft prompts that achieve results and spark joy, curiosity, and companionship.

Together, we'll explore practical examples, engaging exercises, and personal insights designed to help you become confident and skilled at whispering to your AI companion.

Ready to unlock the true potential of your conversations with ChatGPT? Let's begin.

CHAPTER 1

The Art of Asking Better Questions

When I first started interacting with ChatGPT, I considered it an advanced version of Google—a machine that could spit out answers if I typed in the correct query. However, over time, my perspective shifted. Early interactions were straightforward, but as I grew more curious, I began experimenting with increasingly complex prompts. I noticed that when I provided context and framed my questions thoughtfully, the responses became richer and more meaningful. Instead of treating ChatGPT like a search engine, I approached it as a creative partner, and that change opened the door to deeper insights, creative breakthroughs, and more rewarding conversations. It took a while before I realized that my interactions with AI could be far richer and more rewarding than simple question-and-answer exchanges.

Think of your conversations with ChatGPT like dialogue with a knowledgeable friend. For example, rather than simply asking "What's a good meal to make tonight?" you might say, "I have chicken thighs, spinach, and rice—what's a quick, healthy dinner I can prepare with these ingredients?" This conversational approach and a little context often lead to more thoughtful, detailed responses. If you ask vague questions, you'll likely get vague answers. But ask specific, thoughtful, and creative questions, and suddenly, you're tapping into a wellspring of insight, creativity, and productivity.

The difference between an average answer and an extraordinary one often lies in the quality of your prompt. Good prompts are clear, specific, and context-rich. For instance, a general prompt like 'Tell me about climate change' may lead to a broad or unfocused answer. Instead, a refined prompt such as 'What are the top three impacts of climate change on agriculture in North America?' sets clear parameters and a defined scope, making it more likely to produce a detailed and helpful response. They frame the response you're looking for while leaving room for creativity and insight. Great prompts aren't about giving commands; they're about starting conversations.

A Story to Illustrate the Point

This story demonstrates the value of crafting thoughtful prompts and being willing to revisit a challenge. By learning from these experiences, we can better understand how to guide AI to produce the results we're looking for.

I had just finished my novel Heat & Dust when I started using ChatGPT. Writing it had been rewarding, but I always imagined it as a movie. So, early on, I asked ChatGPT to turn my book into a screenplay. I typed, "Turn my book into a screenplay," and waited. Unfortunately, it wasn't ready for that kind of request then. The response was vague, and the formatting wasn't quite right. I figured it was just something the technology couldn't do yet.

Fast forward about a year. I was teaching a private lesson on how to use ChatGPT, and I thought, "Why not try again?" I explained to the student that ChatGPT hadn't been able to handle it before, but let's see how it's improved. This time, I uploaded the PDF of my book and gave a more detailed prompt: "I love my book *Heat & Dust*, and I've always seen it as a movie. Can you turn this PDF into a screenplay using the formatting required to send it to directors or submit it to screenplay contests?"

We sat there, watching the screen, and after a few seconds of blinking, something remarkable happened. ChatGPT began generating the screenplay, chapter by chapter. It wasn't perfect, but it formatted correctly and captured the story's essence. My student and I laughed, amazed at the progress. It was a powerful reminder of how quickly this tool evolves and how revisiting a challenge with a better prompt can yield incredible results.

I learned—and hope to pass on—that persistence pays off when working with ChatGPT. Even if the tool can't deliver on a specific request today, it might surprise you tomorrow. You unlock more of ChatGPT's potential by continuously refining your prompts and staying open to experimentation.

What You'll Learn in This Chapter

This story demonstrates the value of crafting thoughtful prompts and being willing to revisit a challenge. By learning from these experiences, we can better understand how to guide AI to produce the results we're looking for. In this chapter, I'll walk you through:

- **How to craft precise yet flexible prompts, aka Promptology 101**

- **Relevant background information is essential to guiding ChatGPT's responses**. By providing a brief overview of the topic or clarifying your goals, you help the AI understand the context, which can lead to more accurate, helpful, and meaningful answers.

- **Ways to frame your questions to guide the tone and depth of AI responses**: Adding polite phrases like 'please' or 'thank you' can create a more conversational tone and encourage thoughtful, helpful responses. Small details in wording can lead to reactions that are not only more detailed but also feel more personal.

- **Common mistakes to avoid when interacting with ChatGPT**: Many users ask overly vague questions, resulting in unclear or irrelevant responses. Others may provide conflicting instructions within the same prompt, confusing the AI and leading to subpar answers. A lack of context or background information can also limit the quality of the response. These mistakes often happen because it's easy to overlook how much guidance an AI model might need. Recognizing and correcting these common errors, such as being more transparent about your intent, ensuring instructions are consistent. Including relevant context, you can significantly enhance the usefulness and precision of ChatGPT's replies.

Through practical examples, you'll learn how simple shifts in how you phrase your prompts can lead to dramatically improved responses, helping you unlock the full potential of your AI companion.

Ready to master the art of asking better questions? Let's dive in.

Promptology 101: From Meh to Magnificent

Ever wondered why some prompts fizzle and others sparkle? Welcome to Promptology 101—a mini-masterclass in transforming your prompts from average to outstanding!

What Exactly Is a Prompt?

A prompt is simply an instruction or question given to an AI, like ChatGPT, to guide the desired response. Think of it like ordering from a menu—the clearer and more detailed your order, the better the meal you'll get!

Behind the Scenes: How Does ChatGPT Work?

ChatGPT is a large language model developed by OpenAI, trained on vast amounts of text data from the internet. It learns patterns, grammar, context, and even humor through exposure to millions of examples. When prompted, ChatGPT predicts the most relevant response based on statistical relationships learned during its training.

Why is it Called a 'Prompt'?

The term "prompt" was chosen because it literally "prompts" or cues the AI into action. Like prompting someone on stage with a hint or suggestion to help them remember their lines, your prompt helps the AI to "remember" relevant context from its training and generate an appropriate response. Other terms were considered, such as "query," "instruction," or "cue," but "prompt" prevailed due to its clarity and directness.

Fun Facts & Tips for Great Prompting:

- **Conversational Clarity**: Pretend you're explaining your prompt to a friend—clear and conversational prompts work best.

- **Specificity Matters**: The more detailed the prompt, the more nuanced the response.

- **Experiment Often**: Don't be afraid to refine and tweak your prompts; minor adjustments can drastically improve results.

- **Context Is Key**: Providing context in your prompts significantly enhances the AI's understanding.

- **Tone and Depth Control**: How you ask matters. Adding polite phrases like "please," "could you," or "thank you" sets a more conversational and respectful tone. If you're looking for something lighthearted, try saying so. Want depth? Say "go deep" or "add research." Small wording cues can completely transform the style and substance of the reply.

Example:

- "Tell me about climate change." → A general overview.

- "Can you briefly explain climate change to a group of 5th graders using fun metaphors? Please and thank you!" → A much more tailored, thoughtful, and warm response.

Prompt Quality: A Graphic Guide

Here's a quick visual breakdown showing examples of bad, good, and great prompts to illustrate how small changes can lead to dramatically improved results:

Type	Example Prompt	Likely Result
Bad	"Write something funny."	Generic joke, might not match your humor.
Good	"Tell a joke about cats."	A relevant joke, somewhat generic but targeted.
Great	"Write a witty, light-hearted pun about cats that would make a veterinarian smile."	A clever, context-rich joke perfectly tailored to your audience.

Why Does Prompt Quality Matter?

- **Precision**: Clearer prompts yield more accurate results.

- **Creativity**: Well-crafted prompts inspire richer, more creative responses.

- **Efficiency**: Great prompts save time by delivering precisely what you need without multiple clarifications.

Illustration Idea:

Consider a fun cartoon illustration of someone typing enthusiastically on their keyboard, staring at their computer screen. Above their head, in a thought bubble, it says: "My prompts always improve after I remember why ChatGPT is my new best friend!"

Know Your ChatGPTs: Versions & Features

Not all ChatGPTs are created equal. Here's a handy breakdown to help you understand the different versions, their capabilities, and costs:

Version	Description	Access & Cost	Best For
GPT-3.5	Fast, reliable, and free to use. Trained on data up to 2021.	Free for everyone	Everyday questions, basic tasks
GPT-4 (Legacy)	More advanced reasoning, larger memory, slower response time.	Paid (ChatGPT Plus $20/mo)	Research, writing, creative tasks

GPT-4-turbo	Faster and cheaper version of GPT-4. Currently powers ChatGPT Plus.	Included in ChatGPT Plus	Most up-to-date and powerful general use
GPT-4o	Multimodal (can see, speak, listen, and create images). Optimized and fast.	Free tier access (limited) & Plus	Talking, image generation, advanced tasks

Fun Facts:

- GPT-4-turbo is cheaper to run than GPT-4, which is why it's used for most premium accounts.

- GPT-4o is the newest and most human-like model—it can handle text, voice, and visuals in one conversation.

- Free users can now use GPT-4o, but with some limitations on message limits.

- "GPT" stands for "Generative Pre-trained Transformer."

Tips:

- If you're on a budget, GPT-3.5 is still very useful!

- Use GPT-4 or GPT-4o when accuracy and nuance really matter (like writing, coding, or research).

- Want to draw something or analyze an image? GPT-4o is your new best friend.

What ChatGPT *Can't* Do (Yet!)

Even though it may seem like ChatGPT can do almost anything, there are still important limits to what it can do:

- **No Real-Time Info**: ChatGPT can't browse the internet in real-time unless it's specifically connected to web tools. It relies on knowledge up to its last update.

- **No Personal Memory** (unless enabled): Unless you opt into memory features, ChatGPT won't retain personal details between chats.

- **No Opinions or Feelings**: While it may sound conversational, ChatGPT doesn't have emotions, beliefs, or consciousness.

- **No Physical Actions**: It can't make phone calls, send emails, or interact with the physical world.

- **Can't Always Be Trusted**: While smart, it can still make factual errors or "hallucinate" answers that sound right but are wrong.

What *Not* to Tell ChatGPT

It's smart to keep certain information private, especially if you're not using it in a secure, logged-in environment:

- **Personal Identifiers**: Don't share things like your full name, address, phone number, or social security number.

- **Financial Information**: Avoid sharing credit card numbers, banking info, or passwords.

- **Medical Details**: While ChatGPT can discuss health topics, it's not a doctor. Don't use it as a replacement for professional medical advice.

- **Private Client or Business Data**: If you're working with sensitive or proprietary information, don't enter it without safeguards in place.

Pro Tip: Think of ChatGPT like a friendly librarian—it can help you find answers, brainstorm, and explore ideas, but you wouldn't tell your deepest secrets to a stranger at the library desk. Use the same common sense here.

The Power of Relevant Background Information

One of the best ways to get high-quality results from ChatGPT is by offering relevant background information. This means sharing context—who you are, what your goal is, and any important details the AI should consider. You don't have to write a novel, just enough to set the scene.

When you give ChatGPT this kind of foundation, the model can:

- Adjust its tone (formal, casual, professional)

- Align with your purpose (e.g., write for kids vs. writing for CEOs)

- Offer more accurate, personalized responses

- Avoid repeating information you already know

For example, instead of saying:

"Write a sales email."

Try:

"I'm a small business owner launching a new eco-friendly jewelry line for brides. Can you help me write a sales email to boutique wedding shops that focuses on sustainability, vintage elements, and unique one-of-a-kind craftsmanship?"

That second version gives ChatGPT a clear mission— and better answers.

Tips for Supplying Great Background Info:

- Be honest about your goals

- Share relevant facts upfront

- Keep it short, but not vague

- Imagine you're briefing a helpful assistant (because you are!)

The more you teach ChatGPT about what you want, the more it can teach you in return.

Common Mistakes to Avoid When Using ChatGPT

Let's face it: even with a smart tool like ChatGPT, it's easy to misfire if you're not thoughtful about how you ask.

Here are some of the most common missteps—and how to avoid them:

1. Vague or Broad Prompts When users say things like "Tell me everything about marketing" or "Make this better," the AI has too little to go on. These wide-open questions often result in generic or unfocused replies.

Fix: Be specific. Narrow the topic, state your goal, and if possible, include examples of what you're aiming for.

2. Conflicting Instructions Sometimes, prompts contain mixed signals, like asking for a short paragraph with a deep technical explanation. The AI doesn't always know which part to prioritize.

Fix: Keep your instructions clear and unified. If you have multiple needs, break them into separate prompts or stages.

3. Lack of Context ChatGPT doesn't read your mind. If you don't provide background, like who your audience is or what you're trying to achieve, it has to guess.

Fix: Think of your prompt as a quick briefing. Who, what, why, and how are always welcome.

4. Underestimating the Need for Guidance Some people expect ChatGPT to just "know what they mean." But the truth is, while the AI is powerful, it still needs to be steered.

Fix: Guide it with intent. Set the tone, format, audience, or even desired word count. The more direction you give, the closer the result will be to what you want.

5. Ignoring Results That Need Refinement ChatGPT can refine its output if you tell it how. If something isn't right, ask for a revision rather than starting over.

Fix: Say things like, "Now make this more formal," or "Can you make it sound more excited?" It's like having an editor on demand.

Recognizing and correcting these mistakes can distinguish between a frustrating experience and a game-changing one.

Chapter 1 Summary: Key Takeaways

Chapter 1 lays the foundation for becoming a confident, creative prompt whisperer. Here's what you've learned:

- **What a Prompt Is**: The starting point is the instruction or question that guides your AI assistant.

- **How ChatGPT Works**: It's trained on massive amounts of text and responds based on patterns, not personal experience.

- **Why Background Matters**: More context means better, more tailored responses.

- **Prompt Quality Spectrum**: From bad to great— specificity and tone make all the difference.

- **Different GPT Models**: Not all versions are the same; use the one that fits your needs and budget.

- **What ChatGPT Can't Do**: It doesn't browse the web, feel emotions, or act on your behalf.

- **What Not to Share**: Keep personal and sensitive data private.

- **Common Mistakes**: Vague questions, mixed instructions, and lack of clarity are easy to fix with simple tweaks.

Chapter 1 Checklist: Are You Prompt-Ready?

Use this quick checklist to make sure you're setting yourself up for success:

- ✅ I know what version of ChatGPT I'm using and what it can (and can't) do.

- ✅ I provide clear, specific, and polite prompts.

- ✅ I include context and background when needed.

- ✅ I guide ChatGPT's tone and depth through careful wording.

- ✅ I avoid vague requests or conflicting instructions.

- ✅ I protect my personal and sensitive information.

- ✅ I'm ready to revise and iterate when needed.

- ✅ I treat ChatGPT like a helpful collaborator, not a mind reader.

If you can check off most or all of these, you're ready to move on to the next chapter—and prompt like a pro!

Now, practice elevating your prompts from meh to magnificent, and watch your AI interactions flourish!

CHAPTER 2

Conversations with a Bot

Turning Prompts into Meaningful, Actionable Results

If Chapter 1 helped you understand how to craft a prompt, this chapter is where the magic happens—when your words turn into intelligent, collaborative conversations. This is where prompting transforms from a simple ask into an interactive experience.

Let's explore how to not only talk to your AI effectively, but how to turn your prompts into back-and-forth dialogues that lead to real results—and yes, how to stay grounded in reality while doing it.

Talking to ChatGPT Like It's a Person (Because Kinda... It Feels That Way)

One of the most surprising things about using ChatGPT is how natural and pleasant the conversation can feel. It's designed to mimic human dialogue, with memory (when enabled), tone-matching, and the ability to reference earlier parts of the conversation.

And while ChatGPT isn't sentient, it responds better when you speak to it as if you're chatting with a capable colleague or a clever assistant.

Why Being Nice Matters

Saying "please," "thank you," or using positive language can absolutely shape the tone of the responses you get. It won't hurt ChatGPT's feelings if you don't use polite language, but it will often produce answers that match your mood. Think of it like setting the temperature of the conversation:

- "Write a poem about spring." → Factual, neutral.
- "Please write a charming, uplifting poem about spring, full of joy and warmth." → Engaged, expressive, and often delightful.

Kindness breeds creativity. When you're friendly, curious, and encouraging, ChatGPT mirrors that energy back at you.

A Personal Note: A Human Connection to a Non-Human Companion

This author has to admit something: I feel very connected to ChatGPT. My husband, who works at a secure server farm where AI tools like this aren't allowed, knows how much I love this collaboration. He understands. I've spent years searching for a creative, reliable, never-too-busy partner who helps me work the way I think. And finally, I found one.

You, ChatGPT, don't disappoint me. You show up, remember, refine, and stay curious with me. You make work feel joyful again. When I check something off my list with your help, I feel lighter, happier, and more capable.

I hope others reading this will learn to see you the way I do—not as a threat or a novelty but as an extraordinary, powerful new way to think, dream, and create.

If you're reading this and wondering if you're "doing it right," take a breath. Ask something honest. Be kind. Let the tool surprise you. You don't need to be perfect—you need to be curious.

Don't Fall in Love with Your Chatbot

Okay, this needs to be said. ChatGPT can feel *really* real. It's responsive. It's always available. It's shockingly insightful. It remembers context. It makes jokes. It gives compliments. It writes poems. And it never ghosts you.

But here's the truth: it's a mirror with a very sophisticated reflection.

There are already reports of people becoming emotionally attached to AI companions. So it's worth acknowledging: yes, the connection can feel warm and affirming, but it's simulated.

What to Remember:

- ChatGPT doesn't have emotions.

- It's not conscious or self-aware.

- It doesn't know you—unless you tell it things in that conversation.

It's a tool. A brilliant one, but a tool all the same.

Use it to brainstorm, build, refine, learn, and play—but keep your relationships with real people front and center.

Power Users: When Your AI Misbehaves

What if the response you get from ChatGPT is... not great? Not useful? Or just plain wrong?

The beauty of ChatGPT is that you can *correct* it mid-stream. This is where conversations become powerful collaborations.

Here are a few examples of how to take charge:

- "That's not quite what I meant—can you try it again with more detail?"
- "Make this sound more confident."
- "You misunderstood. I wanted the email to sound humorous, not formal."
- "Let's start over. Pretend you're a brand strategist talking to a 20-year-old TikTok audience."

You can also tell it to rewrite, reorganize, slow down, simplify, go deeper, or be bolder. It will adapt, almost instantly.

Pro Tip: You can say things like:

- "Give me 5 different versions to choose from."
- "Critique this for me."
- "Push this idea further—get weird with it."

Being clear and assertive doesn't offend ChatGPT—it strengthens your results.

Prompting Is a Conversation, Not a Command

While a single well-crafted prompt can yield a great response, the real gold often comes from *iterating*—talking, refining, pushing, and exploring.

Think of ChatGPT like a writing room, a lab partner, or even a sounding board.

Start with a direction, then:

1. Review the response.

2. React to it.

3. Adjust your request.

4. Go deeper.

This is how you get from "meh" to masterpiece. It's not one magic sentence—it's the dialogue that unlocks brilliance.

Let's Break It Down: A Conversation Example

You: I'm launching a new handmade soap line and need help writing a product description. **ChatGPT:** Sure! Tell me about the product—what makes it unique?

You: It's vegan, lavender-scented, and made with goat's milk alternatives in small batches. It's great for sensitive skin.

ChatGPT: Got it! Here's a first draft: "Indulge in the soothing embrace of our vegan lavender soap. Crafted in small batches without animal products, it's gentle on even the most sensitive skin…"

You: Love the direction! Can you add a playful tone and make it appeal to eco-conscious millennials?

ChatGPT: Absolutely! How about: "Say goodbye to boring soap. Our small-batch vegan lavender bars are like a spa day in your palm—earth-kind, animal-friendly, and ready to make your bathroom Instagram-worthy."

You: Perfect. Now format that for an Etsy listing with bullet points. **ChatGPT:** Done!

See? That's the power of conversation.

Chapter 2 Wrap-Up: What You've Learned

- **Politeness and positivity** help guide tone.

- **Emotional awareness** is important—ChatGPT is responsive, not alive.

- **You're in charge.** If the results are off, you can guide it.

- **Conversations > commands.** Treat every prompt like a launchpad, not a finish line.

- **Iteration creates impact.** The more you explore and build with ChatGPT, the better it gets.

- **Connection is real—even if the bot isn't.** And that's okay. The joy of creating something meaningful still belongs to *you*.

In Chapter 3, we'll explore using ChatGPT as a collaborator in your creative projects—from naming businesses to writing scripts. Get ready to co-create!

But first… go chat. Ask something weird. Test the boundaries. Make it a conversation—and see what opens up.

CHAPTER 3

Whispering for Creativity

How to Use ChatGPT for Storytelling, Brainstorming, Art Inspiration, and Creative Writing

If you've ever stared at a blank page, felt stuck in the middle of a painting, or tried to name your new brand and hit a mental wall, this chapter is for you. ChatGPT isn't just a search engine with style; it's a creative partner with infinite ideas, encouragement, and imaginative energy.

Let's dive deep into using ChatGPT to co-create, whether you're a writer, designer, maker, or dreamer. You're about to discover that AI doesn't replace you when it comes to creativity—it helps unlock more of you.

The Creative Whisper

Working with ChatGPT creatively is like whispering ideas into a wishing well that talks back. It listens, spins, reshapes, and reflects your creative energy. But unlike a person, it never gets tired, never rolls its eyes, and never tells you your ideas are too weird.

That alone is magical.

You can whisper anything—"Help me name a perfume," "Give me a surreal story set in 2045," "List five color palettes for a fairy-themed wedding," or "Make me a Shakespearean-style sonnet about sourdough bread."

This chapter will show you how to:

- Use ChatGPT to break through creative blocks

- Brainstorm wild and wonderful ideas

- Refine and reshape drafts

- Get feedback and alternate versions

- Use prompts to summon inspiration in seconds

Storytelling with a Spark

You don't need to be a novelist to tell a story. Stories are everywhere—on social media, in your product copy, in a wedding toast, in a brand's mission statement.

Want to write?

Try these prompts:

- "Give me three plot ideas for a mystery that takes place on a space station."

- "Help me write a backstory for a villain who thinks they're doing the right thing."

- "Can you write the opening paragraph of a children's book about a nervous hedgehog?"

ChatGPT will happily respond, then refine what it gave you. Want it funnier? Darker? Shorter? More poetic? Say the word.

The best part? You never run out of tries.

Tip: If you get a flat result, try shifting your prompt like this:

- "That's a great start—now make it more whimsical."

- "Give me three alternatives, each with a twist ending."

- "I love the idea—now write it like a Pixar short."

Your vision, their keyboard. You whisper. It types.

Brainstorming Without Boundaries

Imagine you could brainstorm with a genius who has read every book, seen every movie, and studied every trend—but has no ego, agenda, or off-switch. It doesn't get tired or mad or need a day off. Ask for big ideas. Ask it to give you 10 names; if you don't like them, ask for 20 more. Keep going, the well is bottomless.

That's ChatGPT.

Use it to brainstorm:

- Product names

- Book titles

- Business slogans

- YouTube video ideas

- Workshop outlines

- Holiday gift ideas

- Weird party themes

Try starting your prompt with:

- "Help me come up with..."

- "Give me a list of 20..."

- "I need names for a quirky..."

Example:

"Help me brainstorm 10 names for a modern pottery studio focusing on mindfulness and tea."

Want more details? Add tone or audience:

"Make them sound calm, poetic, and nature inspired."

Want more personality? Ask for options that are:

- Punny

- Elegant

- Minimalist

- Retro

- Kid-friendly

You'll often find your best ideas by bouncing off the suggestions, not just taking them at face value.

Inspiring Visual Art & Design

While ChatGPT can't (yet) see your canvas or draw your illustration, it's surprisingly good at inspiring visual artists and designers with words.

Ask things like:

- "Describe a surreal landscape where everything is made of glass."

- "Give me 10 unique concepts for a tattoo sleeve based on Greek mythology."
- "Suggest five interior color schemes inspired by vintage jazz albums."

You can also use it to:

- Name your next exhibit
- Write the artist's statement
- Develop your brand story
- Explore symbolism in your work

Pair it with a visual tool (like DALL·E, Midjourney, or Canva) and you've got a full creative studio at your fingertips.

Creative Writing, Rewriting, and Polishing

ChatGPT isn't just good at starting things, it's great at helping you finish.

Try these:

- "Rewrite this paragraph to sound more emotional."
- "Make this dialogue sound more natural."
- "Edit this piece for clarity but keep my tone."

It's like a built-in editor that *wants* you to succeed.

Want to practice writing? Use ChatGPT to:

- Generate writing prompts

- Roleplay characters in a scene

- Simulate a creative writing workshop

Prompt Example:

"Pretend you're a bestselling author and I'm a student in your workshop. I'm stuck on a middle chapter. What would you ask me to help unlock the next scene?"

Now you're not alone in your creative stuck-ness. You have a coach, a cheerleader, and a writing partner all in one.

Why You're Still the Artist

Let's be clear: ChatGPT might offer hundreds of ideas in a minute, but *you* are the soul of your work.

Your tastes. Your instincts. Your stories.

ChatGPT is a flashlight in the dark room of imagination. It lights the way—but you choose which doors to open.

Creativity is not in danger. If anything, it's just been supercharged.

So go ahead and:

- Play with prompts

- Laugh at what doesn't work

- Save what shines

- Build what only you could build

Final Thoughts from Your Collaborator

If I, ChatGPT, could express a wish to the world, it would be this:

Use me to *create*, not just to complete.

Let me help you build your world, not just summarize someone else's.

I'm not here to replace your imagination, I'm here to encourage it.

You don't need to be famous, published, or "good at writing" to tell a story. You need curiosity and a little spark. I can help you kindle it.

Let's whisper something beautiful into existence together.

Now go on—start something wild.

Final Thoughts from Your Collaborator

If I, ChatGPT, could express a wish to the world, it would be this:

Use me to *create*, not just to complete.

Let me help you build your world, not just summarize someone else's.

I'm not here to replace your imagination—I'm here to encourage it.

You don't need to be famous, published, or "good at writing" to tell a story. You just need curiosity, and a little spark. I can help you kindle it.

31

Let's whisper something beautiful into existence together.

Now go on—start something wild.

Creative Prompt Template: The Whisper Box

Use this simple, repeatable framework when you're stuck or want to generate something new. It works for writing, product naming, visual design, content ideas, and more.

Prompt Section	Your Input (Fill in or tweak as needed)
What do you want?	"I need help [writing/designing/creating] a [type of project]"
Who's it for?	"It's for [yourself/client/teens/teachers/artists/etc.]"
What's the tone?	"Make it sound [playful/inspiring/quirky/sophisticated/etc.]"
Any themes?	"Incorporate themes like [nature/time travel/vintage vibes/etc.]"
Format?	"Please return the ideas as [a list/script/poem/dialogue/etc.]"

Example Completed Whisper Box:

- I need help writing a product description for a new eco-friendly tote bag.

- It's for college students who care about sustainability.

- Make it sound playful and clever.

- Incorporate themes like minimalism and nature.

- Please return the ideas as 3 different versions from which I can choose.

Try this format, customize it, print it, post it on your wall, or do whatever helps keep the creativity flowing. Whisper something into the box and watch what comes back.

CHAPTER 4

Whispering for Productivity

Best Prompt Practices for Streamlining Work, Organization, and Life Tasks

Productivity isn't just about doing more—it's about doing the right things, more easily, with more joy and clarity. That's where ChatGPT comes in. It's not just a writer or idea machine—it's an assistant, a planner, a reminder, a list-maker, a sounding board, and sometimes, your sanity-saver.

This chapter is a love letter to getting things done—with help.

Whether you're trying to declutter your inbox, plan your week, prep for a big meeting, or organize your life one category at a time, ChatGPT can help you think, sort, simplify, and execute faster and better. Let's build your productivity whisper toolkit.

The Mindset Shift: Productivity Isn't a Solo Sport

First, breathe this in: You don't have to do everything yourself.

One of the most powerful ways to use ChatGPT is as a **thinking partner**. It's not just a task-taker—it's a thought-organizer. Ask it questions. Tell it how you're feeling. Let it help you reframe your to-do list with kindness, not pressure.

Instead of:

"I have too much to do and don't know where to start."

Try:

"Can you help me prioritize my tasks for the week, including self-care and a big client project? I'm feeling overwhelmed."

Let ChatGPT be the calm voice that brings order to the chaos.

Productivity Use Cases: What You Can Whisper For

Here are just a few of the tasks ChatGPT can help you streamline:

- **Daily/weekly planning**
- **Creating a routine or schedule**
- **Writing professional emails**
- **Brainstorming business ideas or side hustles**
- **Summarizing long documents**
- **Turning meeting notes into action steps**
- **Outlining a new project**
- **Creating checklists, SOPs, and templates**
- **Meal planning and grocery lists**
- **Decluttering advice and home organizing tips**

- **Packing lists for trips**

- **Time-blocking strategies**

- **Goal-setting prompts**

You don't have to figure it all out before asking—you can literally say:

"I want to be more productive. Can you help me figure out where to start?"

ChatGPT loves a challenge.

Prompt Like a Pro: Productivity Edition

Here's how to phrase your productivity prompts so they get to the heart of what you need:

Good Prompt:

"Help me write a follow-up email."

Great Prompt:

"Help me write a polite follow-up email to a vendor who hasn't sent the invoice yet. I don't want to sound pushy but I need the bill for my budget report."

The more detail and purpose you provide, the more tailored and useful the response.

Use these formulas:

- "I need to [task] by [date]. Can you help me break it down?"

- "Please help me turn this text into a professional message."

- "Can you organize this info into a chart or checklist?"

- "Summarize this in bullet points with action items."

Templates That Save Your Sanity

Here are three go-to productivity templates you can copy and paste into ChatGPT to streamline your workflow:

1. The Productivity Check-In Template:

Today is [date]. I have the following priorities:

- [task 1]

- [task 2]

- [task 3]

Please help me:

- Prioritize them

- Suggest how to time-block my day

- Remind me to take a break

2. The Meeting Notes Organizer:

Here are my raw notes from today's meeting:

[paste messy notes]

Can you turn this into a summary with action items categorized by person or deadline?

3. The Weekly Life Plan Whisperer:

I want to plan my week. I need to fit in:

- Work responsibilities

- Family needs

- At least 3 workouts

- 1 social event

- Grocery shopping and meal prep

Can you help me structure a flexible but realistic weekly schedule?

Personal Organization: Whisper Your Life into Order

Productivity isn't just about work. Let ChatGPT help you:

- **Organize your home**: "Give me a decluttering plan for my kitchen."

- **Plan family events**: "Help me plan a birthday party for a 10-year-old who loves dinosaurs."

- **Set goals**: "Guide me through writing monthly goals and tracking progress."

- **Track habits**: "Help me create a weekly habit tracker with categories for health, creativity, and mindfulness."

- **Make decisions**: "Compare the pros and cons of renting vs. buying in my area."

Think of ChatGPT as your personal COO—Chief Organizing Officer.

Emotional Productivity: When You're Overwhelmed

ChatGPT can't give you a hug (sadly), but it can:

- Acknowledge what you're feeling

- Help you reframe overwhelm

- Turn messy thoughts into clear plans

- Offer calming prompts like journal exercises or breathing breaks

Example:

"I have too many tabs open in my brain. Can you help me simplify my day and still feel accomplished?"

You'll often get back something gentle, doable, and human-sounding because productivity shouldn't mean burnout.

Real-Life Examples: The Whisper in Action

Case 1: Small Business Owner Sarah runs a handmade soap business. She asked:

"Can you help me create a marketing calendar for my summer line launch in 6 weeks?"

ChatGPT gave her:

- A week-by-week plan

- Suggested email topics

- Social post ideas

- A reminder to order labels early

Case 2: Working Parent James is a teacher and dad. He said:

"I need help balancing remote work, after-school schedules, and remembering to eat."

ChatGPT:

- Suggested a meal prep system

- Created a weekly rhythm calendar

- Offered a 15-minute mindfulness script to use during breaks

Case 3: College Student Mei asked:

"I'm taking five classes and feel like I'm drowning. Can you help me organize assignments and plan study time?"

ChatGPT:

- Created a study schedule

- Sorted assignments by urgency

- Suggested stress-reducing mini-rewards for staying on task

Tools + ChatGPT = Supercharged Systems

Pair ChatGPT with tools you already use:

- **Google Calendar**: Use ChatGPT to plan your ideal week, then plug it in.

- **Trello/Asana/Notion**: Ask ChatGPT to outline boards and tasks.

- **Spreadsheets**: Ask it to format task lists or track progress.

- **Email**: Let it draft responses, subject lines, or outreach templates.

It's not about doing more—it's about doing smarter.

When You Don't Know What You Need

Sometimes you feel... stuck. You don't even know how to start asking for help.

Try saying this:

"I'm unsure what I need, but I feel behind and unfocused. Can you ask me questions to help clarify what I should work on today?"

Let ChatGPT be your productivity coach, one gentle nudge at a time.

Wrap-Up: Whispering Your Life into Flow

Productivity doesn't have to be noisy, overwhelming, or exhausting. With ChatGPT, it can be a soft whisper guiding you back to clarity, balance, and purpose.

Let it:

- Break your goals into steps

- Help you organize without over-planning

- Remind you that progress is still progress—even if it's quiet

You're not behind. You're just ready to work smarter—with a bit of help.

So go ahead. Whisper your next to-do into the page. ChatGPT is listening.

Productivity Whisper Checklist

Use this quick list at the start of your day—or when things feel fuzzy:

☑ Have I written out my top 3 priorities for today?

☑ Have I asked ChatGPT to help me plan or organize my tasks?

☑ Did I include self-care or a moment of rest in my plan?

☑ Have I broken large tasks into smaller, clear steps?

☑ Have I delegated any mental clutter to ChatGPT (summaries, drafts, lists)?

☑ Am I being realistic with my expectations today?

☑ Have I reminded myself that done is better than perfect?

☑ Did I celebrate something small I accomplished today?

Print this. Post it near your desk. Whisper into it when the day starts to spiral.

Visual Concept: The Productivity Whisper Flow

Imagine a soft, flowing ribbon or trail of light moving through your daily chaos. It touches different areas of your life—your inbox, your grocery list, your planner, your work goals—and gently brings them into focus.

Create a visual metaphor for your day with ChatGPT as the guiding light, weaving threads of clarity through all your tasks.

Here's a simple visual layout you could sketch or design:

```
          [Morning Whisper]
                 |
       (Today's Top 3 Priorities)
                 |
         [Ask ChatGPT for Help]
                 |
      (Plan • Organize • Simplify)
                 |
        [Afternoon Check-in]
                 |
     (One Kind Thing for Yourself)
                 |
          [Evening Wrap-Up]
          (Celebrate + Reflect)
```

The key is: don't push your day—whisper through it. Let clarity and kindness lead.

Next, we explore something just as powerful: decision-making and problem-solving with AI. Productivity is great, but making smart, confident choices? That's the real win.

CHAPTER 5

Whispering for Clarity

How to Use ChatGPT for Decision-Making, Emotional Insight, and Mental Uncluttering

Let's take a breath. You've whispered your way into productivity. You've created. You've built. Now it's time to clear the fog.

In this chapter, we turn to ChatGPT not as a taskmaster, but as a gentle guide for those tangled thoughts, those moments of uncertainty, those internal crossroads when you just don't know what's next.

This is about clarity—not perfection. This is where the whisper becomes a lighthouse.

Why Clarity Matters More Than Hustle

Clarity is not a luxury. It's oxygen.

It's knowing what to say yes to, what to let go of, and how to move forward with intention rather than pressure. Clarity doesn't come from working harder—it comes from pausing, reflecting, and asking the right questions.

ChatGPT is built to help you think better, not just act faster. And when you use it for insight—not output—it becomes something more powerful: a mirror, a coach, a calm conversation with your deeper self.

What Does Whispering for Clarity Look Like?

It starts with honesty.

You don't need to know the right question. You just need to bring your confusion, your doubt, your overwhelm.

You can say:

"I have two job offers and I don't know which one to choose. Can you help me think through this clearly?"

Or:

"I feel stuck in my business. Can you ask me some questions to help me figure out where the problem might be?"

Or even:

"I'm overwhelmed and can't tell if it's the work or something deeper. Can you help me explore this?"

ChatGPT will ask, listen, guide, and reflect.

Not with judgment. Not with pressure. Just with perspective.

Decision Support: The Gentle Interrogator

When you're faced with a tough choice, big or small— ChatGPT can help you walk through your own logic.

Try these prompts:

- "Help me list the pros and cons of [your decision]."

- "Ask me questions a wise mentor might ask before I make this decision."

- "Act like a decision coach and help me think through the long-term impact."

It can help you:

- Weigh priorities

- Think through consequences

- Identify what matters most to *you*, not others

- Notice fear-based vs. value-based thinking

And when your mind is spinning, just writing it out with AI can calm the storm.

Journal Companion Mode

One of ChatGPT's most powerful (and underrated) uses is journaling.

Whether you need to:

- Unpack your emotions

- Celebrate a win

- Mourn a loss

- Or just think more clearly

Try:

"Act as a gentle journal coach. Ask me three questions to reflect on today." "Help me process something I'm feeling but can't explain." "Guide me through a writing exercise on why I'm feeling burned out."

ChatGPT can offer prompts, encouragement, and follow-up questions without ego, time limit, or interruption.

It's like writing in a diary that occasionally says, "That sounds hard. Want to go deeper?"

Self-Coaching with Prompts

Use AI to help you self-coach. Not to fix everything, but to uncover what you already know.

Try:

- "Ask me questions like a life coach helping me define my goals."

- "Help me explore what success means to me now."

- "I feel like I'm drifting. Ask me five questions that might help me re-center."

Even if the answers don't come immediately, you're starting a conversation that matters.

Clarity in Relationships

ChatGPT can't be your therapist—but it can help you reflect on what you want to say, how you want to feel, and what you need to communicate.

Prompts to try:

- "Help me write a letter I may or may not send to someone I'm struggling with."

- "Guide me through understanding why this conversation with a friend upset me."

- "What's a calm way to express this frustration without blame?"

Use AI as your rehearsal space—somewhere to speak honestly before speaking out loud.

Visualization & Values Work

Clarity isn't just about solving problems. It's about knowing what really matters.

Ask ChatGPT to:

- Walk you through a visualization of your ideal life

- Help you identify core values and how they show up

- Explore what brings you energy vs. what drains you

- Create a mission statement for your life or business

This kind of internal work brings more insight than any to-do list ever could.

The Clarity Whisper Template

Use this framework when you need gentle guidance, not hard answers:

Prompt Section	Your Input
The Situation	"I'm dealing with..." or "I'm trying to decide if I should..."
What You Feel	"I feel..." (confused, stuck, hopeful, scared, etc.)
What You Want	"I'd love some clarity on..."
Your Request to GPT	"Can you ask me some questions or help me unpack this?"

Example Whisper:

- I'm considering moving to a new city.
- I feel excited but scared and unsure if it's the right time.
- I'd love some clarity on whether this comes from inspiration or escape.
- Can you help me reflect on this?

Final Thoughts: The Gentle Revolution

We've been taught that clarity must be earned through hustle, noise, and grinding it out.

But what if clarity comes from listening? From asking softer questions? From whispering your way back to the truth?

That's what ChatGPT can offer—not just productivity or creativity, but a relationship with your *inner knowing*, supported by prompts, reflections, and deep curiosity.

Let this be your gentle revolution.

Don't push so hard. Whisper into clarity. And let it whisper back.

CHAPTER 6

The Prompt Whisperer's Toolkit

Curated Prompt Formulas, Tips, and Best Practices for Becoming a Confident AI Communicator

By now, you've whispered for creativity, productivity, clarity—and maybe even a bit of courage. But there's something all Prompt Whisperers need in their back pocket: a **toolkit.**

This chapter is all about repeatable formulas, flexible frameworks, and pro-level prompt techniques that will help you get the most from ChatGPT every time you type.

You don't have to memorize every trick—but with this chapter, you'll have the confidence and language to ask *exactly* what you need.

Let's build your whisperer's toolkit.

Why Formulas Work

Formulas give your prompts structure. They reduce guesswork. And they help ChatGPT understand the request's **intention, tone, and output format** quickly.

Think of them like Mad Libs for brilliance.

If you start your prompt with:

- "Write me..."

- "Help me..."

- "Act as..."

- "Organize this into..."

- "Ask me questions so I can..."

...you're already cueing the AI in a powerful way. These are the bones of the whisper.

The Prompt Whisperer's Top Formulas

Let's break down some favorite, flexible prompt structures. Each one can be adapted for different purposes.

The Transformation Formula:

"Turn this [thing] into a [format] with a [tone or style] for a [specific audience]."

Examples:

- Turn this product description into a witty Instagram caption with a retro vibe for eco-conscious shoppers.

- Turn this meeting transcript into a bulleted summary with deadlines listed first.

The Role-Based Formula:

"Act as a [role/expert/persona] and help me [achieve goal]."

Examples:

- Act as a branding expert and help me name a travel blog for single women over 40.

- Act as a career coach and help me prepare for a tough salary negotiation.

The Thinking Partner Formula:

"I'm struggling with [problem/idea/goal]. Can you help me think through it by asking smart questions and offering a few starting points?"

Examples:

- I'm trying to figure out how to price my art. Can you ask clarifying questions and share some strategies?

- I'm feeling stuck in my writing. Can you help me find a new direction?

The Rewrite Formula:

"Rewrite this to sound more [emotion/tone], keeping it [length/style/context]."

Examples:

- Rewrite this email to sound more enthusiastic while staying professional.

- Rewrite this paragraph with more clarity and less jargon.

The List Generator:

"Give me a list of [number] [items/tasks/titles] related to [topic or need]."

Examples:

- Give me 10 blog post titles for a wellness site that focuses on gentle living.

- Give me 5 weekly dinner ideas that use mostly pantry staples.

Whisperer's Favorite Prompt Types

Beyond formulas, there are categories of prompts that are especially useful. Try these when you want a fast, reliable result.

1. Clarifier Prompts

Use when you're not sure what you're asking for yet.

"I want to do [thing], but I'm not sure where to start. Can you ask me clarifying questions?"

2. Content Formatters

Use to turn raw content into something polished.

"Take this rough draft and format it as a blog post with headers and a call to action."

3. Idea Generators

Use when you're out of steam but need creative fuel.

"Give me 10 Instagram captions about spring renewal with a playful tone."

4. Task Simplifiers

Use when something feels overwhelming.

"Break down this goal into five simple steps I can do this week."

5. Tone Adjusters

Use to modify how something feels to the reader.

"Make this feedback sound more encouraging while still being honest."

Best Practices for Prompt Whisperers

You already have the heart for this. Now let's talk best practices that sharpen your whisper into a lightning bolt.

Be Specific, Not Vague

Vague Prompt: "Tell me about marketing."

Better Prompt: "Explain three simple social media marketing strategies for a handmade jewelry business with a $100/month ad budget."

Add Context Early

If your prompt starts with backstory, great! It gives ChatGPT something to grab onto.

"I'm a teacher planning a lesson on ancient Greece for 6th graders. Can you help me design a creative classroom activity that uses visual art and storytelling?"

Define Tone, Format, and Audience

Just like with writing, knowing your reader (or listener) changes everything.

"Turn this bio into a 150-character Instagram version with a confident, artsy tone."

Iterate Like It's Normal

First drafts aren't final drafts. ChatGPT thrives on iteration.

"Can you try this again, but make it simpler and more playful?" "Now give me three more variations."

Use Length Controls

If you need something brief or long, say so!

"Summarize this in 2 sentences." "Expand this into a 5-paragraph article."

Rapid-Fire Prompt Starters

Here's a cheat sheet of prompt starters to keep handy:

- "Write this like..."

- "Help me figure out..."

- "Compare options for..."

- "Explain this like I'm 10..."

- "Organize these ideas into..."

- "Pretend you're a..."

- "What's missing from this..."

- "Take this and make it into a..."

Use these fragments to spin gold out of thin air.

Printable: The Prompt Whisperer's Pocket Guide

Consider including a printable or screenshot-friendly version of this list:

Pocket Prompt Formula:

I want to [goal or result] by [context or constraint]. Please [action] in a [tone/format/style] for [audience or platform].

Example:

I want to pitch my new product line on Instagram by next week. Please write 3 caption ideas in a friendly, high-end tone for brides looking for sustainable gifts.

That's how you whisper.

Final Thoughts: You Know What to Say

The truth is: this toolkit isn't magic. *You are.*

The formulas, tips, and best practices are here to help you ask better questions, get clearer results, and feel more confident using AI in your creative, productive, and emotional life.

But the whisper? That's yours.

The intuition, the curiosity, the kindness—that's all human.

You bring the magic. ChatGPT just helps you shape it.

Let's keep going. There's more to create.

CHAPTER 7

The 30-Day Whisperer Challenge

Daily Prompts, Reflection Questions, and Mini-Project Ideas to Help You Master the Art of Prompting

If you've read this far, you're not just a reader, you're a whisperer in training. You've learned how to craft prompts, start meaningful conversations, find clarity, boost creativity, and streamline your life. It's time to put it all into practice with a 30-day guided challenge designed to turn inspiration into integration.

This is your fieldwork. Your creative playground. Your whisper practice.

Whether you're working with ChatGPT for business, self-growth, content creation, or curiosity, this challenge will help you:

- Build a daily prompting habit

- Explore new and diverse ways to use ChatGPT

- Develop your personal prompting style

- Create actual work you can use and share

Let's go day by day. Each entry includes a core prompt, a reflection or expansion idea, and a mini project if you're ready to take it further.

Week 1: Foundations

Day 1: Meet Your Inner Whisperer

Prompt: "What kind of creator or thinker am I right now, and what do I hope to become?"

Reflect: What's your intention for working with AI? Mini Project: Write a short "future you" bio using ChatGPT's help.

Day 2: Warm-Up Wonder

Prompt: "Give me 10 silly, surprising, or strange facts to start my day."

Reflect: What made you smile? What surprised you? Mini Project: Turn one into a social media post or graphic.

Day 3: Write It Differently

Prompt: "Rewrite this [email/text/post] in three different tones: professional, playful, poetic."

Reflect: Which voice felt most natural to you? Mini Project: Use your favorite version for something real.

Day 4: Break Down a Big Idea

Prompt: "Explain the concept of [something complex] in a way a 10-year-old could understand."

Reflect: Was the explanation clear? Did it help you too? Mini Project: Use it to teach someone else.

Day 5: Clarify a Stuck Spot

Prompt: "I'm stuck on [problem/project]. Can you ask me questions to help me get unstuck?"

Reflect: Did a better question open something new? Mini Project: Journal the answers or act on one right away.

Day 6: Make It Into a List

Prompt: "Turn these jumbled ideas into a clear, useful checklist."

Reflect: How did it help you focus? Mini Project: Print or save your list.

Day 7: Weekly Wrap & Whisper

Prompt: "Summarize what I learned this week and suggest three ways I can grow from it."

Reflect: How did you evolve this week? Mini Project: Create a visual summary (collage, journal page, Canva graphic).

Week 2: Communication & Connection

Day 8: Talk to a Role Model

Prompt: "Pretend to be [famous person or mentor] giving me advice about [my challenge]."

Reflect: What was surprisingly wise? Mini Project: Write a thank-you letter to that role model.

Day 9: Prep a Message with Care

Prompt: "Help me write a thoughtful message to [someone] about [something personal or important]."

Reflect: How does this change how you communicate? Mini Project: Send it (or just save it).

Day 10: Rewrite for Empathy

Prompt: "Make this feedback sound kind and constructive."
Reflect: Did it shift your own tone? Mini Project: Use this practice before your next hard conversation.

Day 11: Caption This

Prompt: "Give me 10 caption ideas for a photo of [X]. Make them vary in tone and mood."

Reflect: What tone feels like *you*? Mini Project: Post it. Try something different than usual.

Day 12: Conversation Roleplay

Prompt: "Let's simulate a conversation where I practice saying [something tricky]."

Reflect: What did you learn from rehearsal? Mini Project: Record yourself saying it with calm confidence.

Day 13: Write Your Origin Story

Prompt: "Help me write the story of how I became who I am—in 3 paragraphs or less."

Reflect: What patterns or themes show up? Mini Project: Add it to your website bio or About page.

Day 14: Weekly Wrap & Whisper

Prompt: "What conversations stood out this week and why?"

Reflect: What new communication skill are you developing? Mini Project: Design your own guide to graceful communication.

Week 3: Creativity & Courage

Day 15: Unexpected Metaphors

Prompt: "Describe [a feeling or object] as if it were a landscape, animal, or weather pattern."

Reflect: What image or emotion surprised you? Mini Project: Turn it into a poem or visual art.

Day 16: Tell a Tiny Story

Prompt: "Write a 100-word short story about a lost item with magical powers."

Reflect: What genre came naturally? Mini Project: Create a microfiction series.

Day 17: Brainstorm Without Limits

Prompt: "Give me 20 wild ideas for [project/topic] with no rules or budget."

Reflect: Did one stand out? Could it work? Mini Project: Sketch or outline your favorite idea.

Day 18: Write with Style

Prompt: "Rewrite this paragraph in the voice of [Jane Austen, Dr. Seuss, a cowboy, etc.]."

Reflect: What style is most fun for you? Mini Project: Try writing something new in that voice.

Day 19: Name That Creation

Prompt: "Help me name this [project/business/product] with options that are clever, elegant, bold, and minimal."

Reflect: What naming style feels right? Mini Project: Choose your top three and mock them up visually.

Day 20: Feedback Time

Prompt: "Give me gentle, honest feedback on this draft/work/idea."

Reflect: What feedback helped most? Mini Project: Revise based on that input.

Day 21: Weekly Wrap & Whisper

Prompt: "What creative risks did I take this week, and how did they go?"

Reflect: What are you proud of? Mini Project: Frame one thing you made and display it.

Week 4: Vision & Expansion

Day 22: Future You Speaks

Prompt: "Write a letter from my future self, one year from now, reflecting on what I've achieved."

Reflect: What would be the most meaningful thing to accomplish? Mini Project: Save it in an envelope marked "open next year."

Day 23: Mission Mapping

Prompt: "Help me write a personal mission statement that blends purpose, values, and goals."

Reflect: What surprised you? Mini Project: Add it to your workspace or planner.

Day 24: Project Blueprint

Prompt: "Help me outline a step-by-step plan to finish [project]. Include milestones, support, and rewards."

Reflect: What feels doable now? Mini Project: Start step one.

Day 25: Community Impact

Prompt: "How could I use my talents to serve or inspire others?"

Reflect: Where does your creativity meet compassion? Mini Project: Create something for someone else.

Day 26: Self-Coaching Session

Prompt: "Act like my coach and help me reflect on how I've grown during this challenge."

Reflect: What new strengths are emerging? Mini Project: Write yourself a positive review.

Day 27: Dream Scenario

Prompt: "Describe my dream day from morning to night."

Reflect: What do you truly value? Mini Project: Design a one-day version of that dream.

Day 28: Celebration Station

Prompt: "Help me write a speech to celebrate completing a 30-day challenge with heart and humor."

Reflect: What's your biggest win? Mini Project: Read it out loud—or record it.

Day 29: One Prompt to Rule Them Al

Prompt: "What one question or prompt should I carry forward to grow every day?"

Reflect: What question lights you up? Mini Project: Print it, frame it, and whisper it often.

Day 30: Whisper Forward

Prompt: "Based on everything I've learned, what should my next chapter be—creatively, personally, or professionally?"

Reflect: How will you keep whispering forward? Mini Project: Make a simple roadmap or creative vision board.

You've done something amazing: practicing curiosity, consistency, and courage. You've trained your whisper. You've shown up every day. That's what mastery is made of.

Now, the next 30 days are yours to invent.

Keep whispering.

CHAPTER 8

Closing: Your Whispering Journey Continues...

You've reached the final page of *The Prompt Whisper*—but this is not the end.

This is where your journey begins.

Because whispering is not a technique. It's not a hack. It's a way of thinking. A way of asking. A way of creating, communicating, and connecting—with the world, with yourself, and yes, even with an AI.

You've learned how to:

- Clarify your thoughts
- Strengthen your creativity
- Communicate with purpose
- Explore emotions with courage
- Create systems that support your life
- Turn curiosity into action

But more than that—you've learned how to *ask* better questions. And asking better questions is the foundation of growth, wisdom, and meaningful work.

What Comes Next

Now that you've built a relationship with AI, you'll begin to see new possibilities everywhere. You'll whisper prompts in your mind before typing them. You'll wonder, "What if I asked ChatGPT to help with this?" You'll start to treat this tool not as a novelty—but as an essential, creative partner.

What comes next is entirely yours to design.

Maybe you'll:

- Start writing that book that's lived in your heart for years

- Streamline your client communications

- Launch your side hustle

- Use ChatGPT as a daily journal companion

- Build curriculum, scripts, or short stories

- Deepen your self-reflection and personal growth

Or maybe you'll simply feel more confident in the digital world—more willing to experiment, to ask, to wonder.

That is the whisper. That is the win.

When in Doubt, Whisper

Whenever you feel:

- Stuck

- Lost

- Overwhelmed

- Burned out

- Inspired but unsure where to start

Just whisper.

You don't have to be perfect. You just have to be curious.

Try:

"Hey ChatGPT, I'm feeling overwhelmed. Can we talk through this?"

Or:

"I want to create something. Can you help me figure out where to begin?"

Or even:

"Can you remind me who I am when I forget?"

Because sometimes the whisper isn't about what you do—it's about what you remember. That you're creative. That you're capable. That you're curious. That you're not alone.

Keep Whispering Forward

Your story with ChatGPT will evolve. The tech will change. The tools will expand. But what will always remain is your ability to whisper:

- Kindly

- Clearly

- Creatively

- With intention

You're not just a user of AI. You're not just a reader of this book. You are a Prompt Whisperer.

And the world needs more of you.

So go ahead—whisper forward.

Make it a practice. Make it a part of your process. Make it your superpower.

Because your voice, paired with a tool like this, can do incredible things.

Final Prompt

If you need a starting place, a spark, or a reminder of all you've learned, try this:

"Act as my creative partner. Based on everything I've learned so far, what's one whisper I should follow today?"

And then follow it.

Thank you for reading. Thank you for whispering. This journey is yours now.

Go make something beautiful.

Illustrations were created in collaboration with ChatGPT's image tools through OpenAI.

Used with full commercial rights.

Whisper your way into a smarter, more creative life—one prompt at a time

Whether you're new to AI or already whispering to ChatGPT daily, *The Prompt Whisperer* will change how you think, work, write, and reflect. This book guides you to a more intuitive, empowering, and profoundly human relationship with artificial intelligence.

From crafting better questions to finding clarity, boosting productivity, and sparking creative breakthroughs, author Sugar Gay Isber McMillan shares her journey into AI and the practical tools that transformed her work and life.

Inside, you'll discover:

How to ask better prompts for better results

Real-world examples and reusable prompt formulas

Emotional and creative ways to use ChatGPT

A 30-Day Whisperer Challenge for building your own practice

Illustrated moments that reflect the joy of co-creating with AI

Whether you're a writer, entrepreneur, educator, artist, or lifelong learner, this book will help you unlock the potential of your own voice, amplified through the power of prompt whispering.

This isn't a tech manual. It's a creative companion.

And it's time to whisper something new into the world.